33 Ways to Sell Your Screenplay!

How to Get Your Screenwriting on the Market and Start a Career as a Screenwriter

by Hal Croasmun

33 Ways to Sell Your Screenplay!

Copyright © 2015 by Hal Croasmun

ScreenwritingU Press

For more information, visit the website: ScreenwritingU.com

Table of Contents

Dedication

This book is dedicated to every screenwriter who has taken the risk of writing and pitching their screenplay. Your courage is inspiring. My hope is that you have the success you desire.

Special Thanks

I'd like to thank the ScreenwritingU Alumni for your never-ending support and belief in me, and for giving me the testing ground to prove the 33 Ways. Thanks goes to Heidi Mastrogiovanni and Ann Kimbrough for going over every chapter of this book with me. Thanks to Dimitri Davis for editing this book. Also, thanks to Karen Mueller Bryson for getting the book ready to publish.

And special thanks goes to my wife, Cheryl Croasmun, the love of my life and inspiration for most of what I do. You never cease to amaze me!

Video: Create Your Own Screenplay Marketing Campaign using 33 Ways!

I'm committed to my writers' success. Since you've joined us by purchasing this book, I'd like to give you a quick video that will dramatically increase your success using the 33 Ways.

This **5 minute video** will give you a visual plan that you can quickly and easily implement as you read the 33 Ways. I hope you enjoy it and achieve the success you want!

Access the video at:

33waysbook.com

Introduction

Early in my career, I asked more than 30 screenwriting teachers a single question:

"How do you sell a screenplay?"

Most of them said something vague like, "You get an agent." And when I asked how you get an agent, they'd shake their head and say something like "You win a contest."

The truth is that they didn't know. But it is not their fault. At that time, people thought that all that mattered was the writing. So they were focused on writing only. Most of them hadn't been in the market, so they just didn't understand that part of the process.

At the time, I was running a corporate training firm and had been designing training programs on leadership, sales, management, and other "soft skill" topics. We had also done business with over 100 major corporations, so I knew there had to be an answer to how to sell a screenplay.

I made it my mission to solve that mystery.

I decided to do what I'm best at—create an "Expert Model." Simply put, an Expert Model is a set of processes and steps to do things at a professional level. The design process entails watching professionals, interviewing them, and synthesizing the model into simple steps that make it easy for someone to perform them. Then testing it, re-interviewing, and solving any problems with the process until it consistently works.

I began interviewing producers. That was twelve years ago.

As of the publishing of this book, I've interviewed:

- 700 producers in Los Angeles,

- 120 agents and managers,

- over 50 studio execs,

- 4 presidents of studios,

- more than 50 readers,

- and more than 100 top screenwriters.

With each interview, I gained another piece of the puzzle.

But having the answers wasn't enough for me, and it isn't enough for you. So three years ago, I brought the ScreenwritingU Alumni together and asked them to join me in this vision:

VISION OF SCREENWRITINGU
To focus on making screenwriting deals
and have as many of our Alumni break
into this industry as possible!

With that as our vision, our Alumni has made over 250 screenwriting deals in the last three years. You can see them at screen writingu.com/success-stories

By the way, I learned as much working with my writers on their deals as I did from the interviews. With many of these deals, I spoke with the writer as they were making the deal. We discussed what was important to the writer, what the producer needed, and the possible strategies for successful negotiation.

I was not their manager or entertainment attorney or agent. I was operating solely from an educational perspective, and in support of my writers.

Eight years ago, I put out a predecessor to this book to 3,000 screenwriters called "33 Ways to Break into Hollywood." They absolutely loved it. But since then, the market has changed, the Internet has changed, and I have at least 10 times more experience marketing screenplays. Because of that, I believe you'll find this book much more useful.

One more thing to remember: marketing yourself and your script is an ongoing process that takes work. It is not a magical process that instantly produces a winning lottery ticket. You create a plan, make smart decisions, take consistent action, and then learn from every one of your experiences.

Do that and you'll succeed.

You can do it.

Hal Croasmun
President
ScreenwritingU

Chapter One:
Marketing Basics Sell Your Scripts

A screenplay can be called many things -- art, story, blueprint, or even the launching point for a blockbuster movie. Whatever you think it is, please know that the moment you begin marketing your screenplay, it suddenly takes on a business purpose.

For a screenplay to sell, it needs to be written in a way that works for the market. These strategies will help you succeed at the Marketing Basics.

Strategy 1. Great Writing Is Required For Your Success

This one has to be #1 on the list. It is the basis for all of the other strategies.

Some people think that their scripts should sell without great writing. They have a tendency to go for "good enough." In fact, some writers actually send out scripts they know are flawed, hoping Hollywood will "see the potential."

Here is both the bad news and the good news.

No one in Hollywood is looking for average writing or "potential."

They want Great Writing!

That is bad news if a writer wants to send in average writing. But it is GREAT NEWS for anyone who is committed to doing the underlying work that will have their screenplay be the very best it can be.

Why is it great news?

Because it means that your writing will stand out!

With 100,000 screenplays coming into Hollywood a year, the competition is very stiff. But what most screenwriters don't realize is that their real competition isn't the contest winners. Their greatest competition comes from already produced writers who are constantly looking for work.

How do you know if the quality of your screenplay is high enough? Here are four sources that can help you gauge the quality of your work:

- Compare your script to the best produced screenplays.

- Enter high level contests to see how your script fares.

- Script coverage.

- The initial response of the market to your script.

At the minimum, a producer needs to look at your script and say:

"This is a professionally written script and a professional writer."

Once your script has passed those tests, then start pitching it freely to producers and you'll instantly see if you made the grade. If a producer loves your writing, they'll contact you... even if they don't want this script. Producers want to be connected to great writers.

More than any other skill in this series, quality writing can make the biggest difference for getting you a sale and a career. It is worth doing whatever you have to do in order to become a great writer.

You can do this. And it is worth doing!

Strategy 2. Understand the Rules of this Spec Industry

There are many metaphors applied to selling screenplays. Some people think it is a "lottery" where they send their script in and win a million dollars. Some think it is a "corporate job" where you apply for a position and get it. Others assume they're going to "take it by storm" by showing their brilliance.

While each of those metaphors work sometimes, the truth is that none of them address the most important business aspect of this industry—that it is a "spec" business environment.

What does that mean? In this industry, almost everyone is investing their time, money, and creativity, with the hope that it will pay off when the project sells or is made. Producers option scripts hoping they can set it up with a studio or get funding to make it themselves. Agents sign clients hoping they'll be able to get work for that writer, thus getting paid. Actors attach themselves to scripts hoping that the movie will get distribution.

And unproduced screenwriters write screenplays, hoping they can sell them.

How do you succeed in this spec industry?

A. *Come in with something worth speculating on.*

If you are an unproduced screenwriter, this is the most important thing. You need to bring in a project that really does have a chance of selling.

When established producers consider the risk/reward ratio, the more value you can present to them, the more likely they'll work with you.

B. *Build your credibility.*

Credibility can be built by writing a great script, winning contests, receiving a "Recommend" from coverage, getting an insider to recommend you, and in many other ways.

C. *Learn to play the game—honorably.*

Yes, this industry is a unique combination of competition and collaboration. But one of the big keys to success is building your reputation, and that means operating honorably. Don't let the media fool you into thinking that you get ahead by screwing others. You don't. Build a trustworthy reputation and people will want to work with you.

D. *Focus on getting to the finish line.*

Once you have other people (producer, director, actors, etc.) attached to the project, your purpose should be to get this project finished and out there. Don't put up unnecessary stop signs or drag your feet.

If you can get the movie made, the people involved will want to work with you again and again. Why? Because their speculation paid off... and you were a key part of the success!

Understanding that this is a spec industry means you'll come in with an advantage. You'll naturally bring in screenplays that producers will want to take risks on. You'll naturally work with people to get movies on the market. And you'll become a writer who is sought after because you make yourself and other people more successful.

It is a great game that is worth playing.

Strategy 3. Make Sure Your Script is Marketable

You may have heard that "marketing is not part of the creative process." I've even had other screenwriting teachers tell me that it is completely "wrong" for a writer to think about the marketing as they write.

I'm sorry, but anyone who tells you marketing is bad is not living in this century!

If your goal is to succeed as a screenwriter and have your movies made, then your story needs to be a wise investment for everyone who puts time or money into it.

Would you option your script to a producer who didn't care about marketing it? I highly doubt it.

The players in your ultimate success may be money people, producers, agents, managers, directors, studios, or Indie filmmakers. Anyone who is going to take a risk on you and your movie is an investor in your project. Your job is to make sure this investment pays off for them.

It is smart to consider the end result of your efforts. In fact, I promise you that A-List screenwriters think about the market. They also think about great characters, how to entertain an audience, how to express their theme, and many other things as they write. But the "market" is part of every decision for a professional

—and it is totally okay for you to add it to your decision-making process.

What makes a screenplay marketable?

At minimum, make sure you have the following:

A. A High Concept pitch that is designed to HOOK producers.

B. Lead characters that appeal to A-List actors.

C. A transformational journey that we can truly live.

D. Fascinating scenes that make the script a page-turner.

E. An opening that instantly engages us.

F. An ending that creates Buzz with audiences!

And this is incredibly important: it is not what you think is marketable, it is what a producer sees as marketable. So you need to raise your standards in each area above to a producer's level.

For example, anyone can create a character. But very few writers know how to create a character that a major actor would fight to play. These are skills that are worth learning.

The more you know about what makes screenplays marketable, the easier it is to impress producers and make that first deal.

Strategy 4. Take Screenwriting Classes With A Track Record of Deals

There are many excellent screenwriting teachers that can teach you a lot of valuable skills. Many of my writers have worked with other teachers and I'm fine with that. But if you want to break into this industry, let me give you one important piece of advice...

... Look for classes that have a record of making deals.

Why is this so important?

Here's the thing: It is not just about learning how to write; it is about writing and marketing yourself in a way that is attractive to agents, producers, and studios.

The competition is tough, so you need every advantage you can get. The classes you need to take are the ones that have a model for success, which should include marketing your script.

If a screenwriting class doesn't include making deals, then it won't consider what matters to producers, agents, actors, and studios... which means it won't help you break into the industry.

At ScreenwritingU, our primary purpose is to have our writers break into the industry—and we have success stories every single week. Check out our screenwriting deals here: screenwritingu. com/success-stories

Have you already mastered these key components of success for a screenwriter?

- Create a High Concept

- Write a marketable script

- Build characters that will attract actors

- Work within a budget

- Create a successful pitch

- Get in the door

- Make the deal

- Collaborate to stay on the project

- Get representation

- Build your own network of producers

It is vital to become comfortable with each of the processes listed above. You need to be able to flow through them in a capable way without resistance or fear.

Bottom line: If the classes you are taking don't cover the subjects above, very likely, you'll stall out somewhere in the process of trying to break into the industry.

As you know, ScreenwritingU has the top track record in the industry for helping writers break in.

If that is appealing to you, join us. You'll be glad you did.

Chapter Two:
Strategies to Build a Fan Base

With today's social media, it's easy to create a fan base.

But the real question is, "How do you create a RAVING fan base that has enough connections to get you into the industry?"

Strategy 5. Build a Network of Fans for Your Writing!

When asked how he broke into the business, one screenwriter said, "I tried to get anyone I could to read my screenplays. After a while, I started getting fans who loved my scripts. One of them told an unknown actor about a script and she read it. Then, she asked if it would be okay to show it to her manager. He read it and a week later, I sold my first script."

This may sound like a sexy strategy, but I know many screenwriters who broke in because of this strategy. And it is actually easy to implement.

There are three rules to guide you:

> Rule #1: *Don't give an unpolished screenplay to anyone in this industry.*

I know this one would seem obvious, but it is the number one reason that people in this industry don't recommend writers. You see, new writers have a tendency to want their contacts to read their early drafts, hoping to get feedback and encouragement... especially when they meet someone inside the industry.

But instead of helping them, the early drafts kill their reputation before the writer has had a chance to become great. Often the writer wants to get a script to a contact they just met before that contact forgets them. But instead of keeping the contact, the early draft often burns the contact.

Rule #2: *Build the trust of your fan base—by ONLY showing them great writing.*

Your job is to intentionally choose what your fan base sees—and make sure they only experience great writing from you. If you do this one simple thing, you'll condition your network to think of you as a professional screenwriter, rather than a wannabe they can't recommend.

Rule #3: *Let them choose to recommend you.*

We'll talk about how to get recommendations in Strategy 7, but for now, the job is to build their trust and belief in you as a professional screenwriter.

Remember, your job is to build a fan base, not destroy it. If you follow the 3 rules above, you'll consistently hand great screenplays to your network, and sooner or later, they'll feel the urge to recommend you to their contacts.

Over time, as you get more and more people talking you up, the odds are that someone in the business will read your script and bring you inside the Hollywood walls.

By the way, if your writing isn't yet at a professional level, you know where to go, right? Hint: ScreenwritingU.com

NOTE: Our Alumni includes over 250 screenwriters who have made deals. As soon as you join us, you have an "Instant Network." It is a great group to have on your side.

Strategy 6. Build Both Reputation and Relationship

Like any other business, film industry players like to work with people they know and trust. Reputation and relationships are absolute keys to your success. And the beautiful thing is that you are 100% in charge of how you present yourself.

Here are a few ways to establish yourself as a person to do business with in Hollywood:

- Have highly marketable projects that people want to work on.

- Present your projects in a compelling way that is easy to grasp.

- Always remember that you are there to help them achieve their goal, as well as for them to be part of you achieving your goal.

- Act in a business-like manner. Friendly, but to the point.

- Be conservative with people's time. Time is a major issue in Hollywood.

- Be collaborative, not difficult.

A few things *not to do* if you want to maintain a professional reputation:

- Don't act desperate. Desperate is often interpreted as "stalker."

- Don't make demands that exceed the boundaries of your relationship.

- Don't give anyone a script that isn't the best it can be.

Always remember that each script you bring to producers is a chance to build a better reputation and relationship.

Strategy 7. Get A Recommendation

The movie business thrives on recommendations. But with hundreds of thousands of unknown writers sending scripts to Hollywood, it is almost impossible for the decision makers to consider all of them.

To solve this, they often rely upon people in their network that they trust.

Here's how it works:

You get your script to someone in your network who knows a producer, agent, manager, or studio exec. They read it and absolutely love it. Because the writing is so good, they can't help but recommend it to their contact. If the producer loves it, they'll gain more belief in the person who recommended it, thus putting more trust in their judgment in the future.

That last part is the most important part for you to know—a person recommending your script is putting his or her reputation on the line every time he or she recommends it.

You want every person who recommends you to be proud they did!

HERE'S AN EASY STRATEGY:

Once your script is truly professional, go out to your network and ask them to read 5 pages. If they like it, they'll choose to read the entire script. And if they fall in love with the story, characters, and writing, they will likely recommend it to one of their contacts.

In Strategy 5, we talked about how important it is to build your fan base by having them see great writing from you every time you send out a script.

If you've done that, and you've honored Strategy 6 to build a relationship with them before pitching, you can subtly ask for a recommendation.

TWO CAUTIONS:

1. *Make sure the writing is great before you send it out.* If not, this strategy can easily backfire.

2. *Do not push, argue, or berate them if they don't recommend your script.* That is short-term thinking and will instantly end any chance of that contact recommending you in the future.

If the writing is truly great, they will WANT to recommend you. Giving them a nudge, or saying something like, "And if you like it enough, feel free to recommend it," is totally okay, but if you have to push for a recommendation, there's something missing from the script, the relationship, or the person's relationship with their contact.

Again, take a long-term view here. Maybe this person needs to see a couple of great scripts before they recommend you. Maybe they need to see you having success with another producer first. Maybe they'll come around next year.

Please don't ever kill a contact by demanding they recommend you now!

IMPORTANT: Remember, you are asking people to risk their reputation. Make sure this is a gamble worth taking.

It might seem as if there is some kind of magic to writers who use this strategy well. In reality, it is just a matter of following the simple rules from Strategy 5 and being patient. If your writing is truly great, your fan base will respond in their own time.

Just for fun, take a look at ScreenwritingU's Most Recommended Screenwriters of 2013: **screenwritingu.com/announcements/ screenwritingus-15-most-recommended-screenwriters-2013**

Strategy 8. Meet Producers on LinkedIn, FB, and Twitter

Hollywood has taken to the social networks. It started with some big stars who embraced Twitter (Aston Kutcher, Charlie Sheen, and others), but now almost everyone in Hollywood is on some social network.

The good news is that you can interact with some producers from anywhere in the world. The even better news is it is possible to build relationships and even make deals with producers online— if you consider what is important to them.

WHAT IS THE PROCESS?

1. Find the producer online.

2. Connect with them.

3. Build a relationship BEFORE you blast them with your pitch.

4. When appropriate, present an idea/pitch.

Here's what doesn't work: Meet someone, and instantly pitch them on something that doesn't fit their needs.

Get to know them. What are their likes, passions, and latest projects?

All of that can be done through social media.

HOW ARE YOU IDENTIFYING YOURSELF?

Producers in Hollywood size people up pretty quickly. They are looking to see if you are coming from a professional perspective... and if so, they consider your request.

Here are a few identities that show up in people's requests:

Tourist/fan = Raving about the producer's movies.

Critic = Criticizing their movies.

Stalker = Pursuing without consideration for them.

Beginner = Asking for feedback on their script, submitting projects that don't fit what the producer does, writing long query letters that don't get to the point.

Professional = Build a relationship then present your proposal —and the proposal fits their needs as much as yours.

One caution: *Don't behave like a stalker, a critic, or a tourist.* These are real people, and they don't do business with individuals who fall into any of these categories.

WHERE'S THE FIT?

The natural tendency is to go after as many producers as you can. But you'll have a lot more success if you look for a real "fit," as in, you have something important in common with them, or your project truly fits their company.

Do that and you'll get more responses—and more QUALITY responses.

WHERE CAN YOU FIND PRODUCERS ONLINE?

Twitter and LinkedIn are the easiest places to find them. Facebook takes a little more work because it is more of a "personal" platform.

ON TWITTER

222 Producers You Can follow on Twitter: (While there, follow ScreenwritingU): **twitter.com/ScreenwritingU/lists/producers**

ON LINKEDIN

There are producer groups you can join.

ON FACEBOOK

Search "Producer" for groups with producers.

CONNECT WITH US

While you are searching producers, connect with us, also.

Follow ScreenwritingU at **twitter.com/ScreenwritingU**

"Like" ScreenwritingU at **facebook.com/ScreenwritingU**

Finally, remember the most important part—relationship first, pitch second—and you'll do great at this.

Strategy 9. Six Degrees of Separation— Fishing for the Big Fish

There's a saying, "It's not what you know, but who you know." Six degrees of separation goes many steps beyond that. It's not who you know, but who they know... and who they know, etc. For example, you may know the librarian whose sister is a therapist for the personal assistant to Tom Cruise.

It is a simple theory that was born in 1929 by author Frigyes Karinthy, who published a volume of short stories titled Everything is Different. One of these pieces was titled "Chain-Links." But it became a catch phrase in the 60's. You are no more than six relationships away from anyone in the world. If you know 100 people that means you could possibly have access to 100 networks.

I learned the foundation of networking from Suzanne Lyons and Heidi Wall at Flash Forward in Los Angeles. It has served me well and I've always been thankful to them for sharing their knowledge with me.

Here are three steps that will help you turn current relationships into networking relationships:

1. *Take the time and effort to build strong relationships and credibility.*

The key here is to build the relationship before you need it. Don't meet someone and instantly start trying to access their network. That's rude and ineffective. Develop real relationships and you'll be far more successful when you make requests for access.

2. *Make a Relationship Map of everyone you know who could possibly know someone in the industry.*

Many times, creating this map will uncover hidden treasures in your network. Even if you think you're aware of everyone who has industry contacts, you may want to check. Some people in your network may surprise you. Place yourself somewhere on the map and then organize the names into the categories of people you will need to know to accomplish your project (agents, casting directors, studio execs, financiers, etc).

3. *Ask in a way that makes it easy for them to access their network.*

Avoid the three D's when you ask—*Dumb, Desperate, and Domineering.* None of those traits will increase your chance of success. Consider using something simple like "I've got a story about_____ that I'm sending to producers. Know anyone that might be interested in it?"

Take the time to build relationships, explore who they know, and ask in a considerate manner. Chances are that you may become one of the amazing Hollywood success stories that came from six degrees of separation.

Chapter Three:
Strategies to Get the Good
News Out There

You've written an amazing script. Now, the job is to get it in front of producers. For many people, this has been a boundary they couldn't cross.

This section provides strategies that are within your control, and have the potential to get your script read by Industry pros.

Strategy 10. Know Your Market

The more you know about the market you want to enter, the easier it is to succeed.

This doesn't mean you need to learn ten thousand little details, but that you need to get the broad strokes right.

In general, you want to match up your script to the market that is best for it. That means a market that has a similar budget range (low budget scripts to low budget companies, high budget to major production companies, etc.), similar genres, and that has an audience for your story.

Consider the two opposites of this industry:

Studios: They're set up for big movies that require a huge marketing budget. Their movies are distributed to a "wide audience," so they need to be interesting to the masses. They often put $50 million into a marketing budget, so the movie needs to be able to generate huge box office sales. In general, it doesn't make sense for a studio to get behind a $1 million movie because it doesn't fit their marketing model.

Small Indie Production Companies: Low budget movies that have heart or deliver a message the producer believes in. They usually have a fan base of their own, so they'll look for movies that will be attractive to that fan base. It doesn't make sense for them to make a big budget movie because they can't get distribution for it.

Once you know what market you are aiming for, do some quick research to gain an understanding about who buys screenplays in that market and what they want. Start looking at the specific companies you are going to approach.

In general, you want to look for companies who do similar movies to your script. Go on IMDb.com to see what movies they've done. Many production companies have their own brand. Jerry Bruckheimer does huge action movies. Wes Craven does horror films. Dreamworks does animation. You have a better chance if you are pitching action movies to action companies. The more that you can target companies that match your script and your credibility, the faster you'll succeed.

By doing some simple research, you'll gain enough understanding to interact with them and make better choices. If you want contact info on the companies, go to **IMDbPro.com**.

Strategy 11: Send Out Quality Query Letters

I've heard many people advise screenwriters that query letters don't work. In my experience, they are both right and wrong at the same time.

Over the last 10 years, I've talked with at least 100 producers who read query letters. I've also talked with 100 who say they never read a query letter. As a general guideline, the ones who don't read query letters are at the top of the food chain—studio people and large producers. But when it comes to small producers, my rough estimate is that there are over 1,000 who do look at query letters.

Your job is to find the producers who DO READ QUERY LETTERS.

When your query letter arrives, the subtext of it instantly answers certain key questions. Can this person write? Do they understand the business? Do they have something marketable? Does this project fit my market? If the answer to those four questions is YES, then your script gets requested.

HOW TO WRITE A QUERY LETTER

If you ask any production company intern, they'll tell you that 90% of all query letters are poorly written. They ramble, justify, confuse, and even complain. Luckily, that means your well-written query letter will stand out from the others.

Here are four keys to your success:

1. *Be brief and to the point.*

Your purpose is to get them to request the script. Here, less is more. Say as LITTLE as you can to get that script request.

2. *Hook the reader in the FIRST sentence.*

Don't tell them why this is a great story. Instead, hook them with something surprising from the story. Then follow that with a one paragraph synopsis of the story.

3. *Give a one or two sentence bio.*

In your bio, tell them why you are the perfect writer for this script and/or what success you've had in contests and the business. But remember that this isn't a resume. It should get to the heart of your credibility for this project.

4. *Give clear contact information.*

Have as much white space on the page as possible. This isn't about filling up the page. In fact, just the opposite. It is about selling your story in a glance. If you do that, then query letters may be a very successful way of marketing your script.

With query letters, you can target producers who make movies similar to yours, or you can use a service to send a blast to agents, managers, and producers... and if it's well-written, you may become the next Hollywood success story.

Strategy 12: Market Your Script Online

It is absolutely possible to market your screenplays without ever leaving your home.

There are sites that focus all of their attention on getting your script seen by production companies. Some are good, some not so good. For now, we're not making a list of those sites or rating their effectiveness.

But there is one I'll highlight. It is InkTip.

InkTip has a database of over 5,000 producers who look through their site, searching for the next great script. At first, I wasn't sure what I thought about them, but when over 20 of our writers made deals through InkTip, I became very supportive of the site.

On the other side, a lot of it has to do with the quality of your writing, and the marketability of your concept.

Whether you choose InkTip or some other site, there is one major key to your success—writing a logline/synopsis that compels a producer to request your script.

WHAT SELLS MOST AT INKTIP?

Inktip specializes in low-budget, limited locations, limited characters, and high concept scripts. They like single genre or a maximum of two genres, but multi-blended genres don't work as well.

You can also sign up for their newsletter that sends out leads to producers looking for scripts.

THE KEY TO LOGLINE SUCCESS...

The place where most screenplays fail in their marketing is their logline. Many are confusing and uninteresting. But the advice I often give is...

DON'T BE VAGUE!

Far too many loglines start out great and end up so vague that you can't tell what will happen.

Consider this logline: "*In her first week in office, the new President of the United States faces terrorism, a recession, and the shutdown of the entire airline system, but nothing could prepare her for what happens next!*"

Most likely, what happens next is the best part of the movie, but we'll never know what that is. Is it, "the visitation of her hyperactive nephew, Boris?" Or maybe it is, "the first invasion on American soil?" Or could it be, "the murder of her V.P. and the entire cabinet?" It could go in 100 different directions, so it is too vague for anyone to waste time on.

The writer probably thought they were intriguing us. Instead, their logline gets tossed out because they didn't tell us the one thing that might have sold their script. Do you see that?

The job is to find the part that HOOKS us and emphasize that!

Your logline sells the story. Reading it should instantly tell what the conflict is and what the best part is. Do that and you have a far better chance of a script request than someone who is trying to intrigue by being vague, I promise you.

Strategy 13: Create a "Home" on the Web

Most of you have heard the story of how Diablo Cody went from blog writing to an Academy Award for the movie *JUNO*.

Can that strategy work for you? Let's explore it.

Every day, thousands of Hollywood assistants do some kind of research on the Net. They research projects they have, look up contact information, and surf to find out what the latest hot news is that could be turned into a movie.

Every once in a while, they visit a screenwriter's Website... or should I say, the screenwriter's "home."

Here's the thing: If they can't find you on the Web, you don't exist. So you need some kind of home base they can visit and find out about you.

You could have any or all of these:

   - Facebook author's page

   - Website resume site

   - Blog

   - Twitter

   - LinkedIn

Here are a few tips:

1. *The important thing is to be CLEAR and INTERESTING.*

If you are using a blog, write about something engaging. Not screenwriting. Not filmmaking. Most people in this business know more than you on those subjects. Instead, write something that will have you stand out from the hundreds of thousands of other writers out there. Make your subject and POV interesting enough that it hooks the producer into calling you.

Write about the unique things you discovered while researching your script. Write about your experiences with the bomb squad in Iraq (Mark Boal and *HURT LOCKER*). Write about being a stripper (Diablo Cody). Write about "Shit My Dad Says" on Twitter and it becomes a TV series (Justin Halpern). They're all interesting!

2. *Write the site with personality and humor.*

Remember, having a "voice" is a big thing in Hollywood. If you entertain the visitor from the first sentence on your site, you'll create the kind of buzz you need to draw the attention you want.

3. *Present yourself as a pro.*

If you are going to put up a scene from your screenplay, make sure it is absolutely amazing writing. So many writers kill their chances by putting up "average writing."

4. *Provide contact information.*

If they can't find you, they can't option your script.

5. *Once you have your site up, market it.*

Put up interesting articles and promote them through your other social networks. Put a one-sentence pitch in the signature file of every email you send out to let people know about your site.

Do all of the above and you'll build contacts and become known for your writing. Who knows, one day, you may get a surprise email from a production company who loves your stuff. Won't that be an exciting day?

Strategy 14: Select Contests That Get Industry Recognition

Most people choose contests without really thinking about their purpose. They're often throwing early drafts at contests that won't help them accomplish their goals. So the most important thing is to get clear on what you need from a contest and find the contests that fit those specific needs.

There is a lot of value that can come from contests:

- Motivation.

- Real deadlines.

- Light Feedback.

- See how you stack up against other writers.

- Recognition.

- Wins, finals, and semi-final placements that give prizes.

- Expand your network.

- Increase credibility in your writer's resume.

- Being promoted by the contest to their contacts.

My advice: *Choose the contests you enter based upon your plan and you career goals.*

If you are new to screenwriting, small contests are a great way to get encouragement and motivation. If you want inexpensive feedback, look for contests that are known for their feedback.

If you are trying to get your scripts in front of producers, then focus your efforts in three areas:

1. Winning or being a finalist in a contest that will bring you credibility.

2. Finding contests that have Industry players as the final judges.

3. Finding contests that publicize the winners in industry magazines.

Remember, the focus here is breaking into the movie business. If you ask around it doesn't take long to find the names of the top 5 screenwriting contests. But there are some smaller ones that also have judges from major production companies and/or announce the results in *Variety* and *Hollywood Reporter.*

Contests are a tool. Use them wisely.

Strategy 15. Target Small Producers and Indie Producers

Some writers are shocked to find out that a studio won't read their script.

The problem is that studios have billions of dollars at stake. Because of that, they are very concerned about risks of any kind. They won't take chances on unknown writers, nor will they risk the possibility that a writer will sue them because they come out with a movie with a similar idea.

What is the solution that can get your movie made?

Small producers. The truth is that there are 10 times more movies made by small producers than by studios. There are also studio movies that started because a writer collaborated up with a small producer who then hooked up with the studio.

And the good news is that small producers answer their own phones and email.

IF YOUR SCRIPT CAN BE DONE ON A LOW BUDGET...

Make a list of five to ten movies that are like yours. Then, go to **IMDb.com** and do some quick research. Looking up the movie, you'll find the name of the producer and director.

If you need their contact information, get a subscription to **IMDbPro.com** where it will give you their address, phone number, and often, their email address.

Some low budget producers are not available on IMDbPro, so you may need to do additional searches on Google to find them.

IF YOUR SCRIPT REQUIRES A HIGH BUDGET...

The strategy here is to go to small producers who are connected to big producers.

You'll do a similar search on IMDb.com, but this time, you'll go to high budget movies. Let's say you look up a big action movie that was done through a studio. You may not be able to get access to the major producer, but if you click on "Full Cast and Crew," you'll see a list of all the producers on the movie. In some cases, there are between 10 and 20 producers on a single movie.

Click on each of the producer names and look for the producer who has the least number of movies made. Why would you go to the smallest producer on that list? Because that producer is part of the network of the major producers and studio.

KEY POINT: Approach producers that are within your reach. Climb the ladder one step at a time. Each step gives you access to the next step.

Use this strategy and you'll gain access to producers who can make your movie. Over time, you'll build relationships until you have an entire network of producers who will read your screen-plays as you complete them.

Chapter Four:
Strategies to Assemble Your A-Team

Why assemble a team? Because it takes a team to get a movie made. It is part of what the movie business is about. You can apply this set of strategies to create a team to get your script sold.

In general, having a team gives you an advantage.

Strategy 16: Get a Script Consultant with Connections

There are two great reasons to use a script consultant who has connections. The most obvious one is the hope that they'll recommend the script to agents and producers. But the other reason may be even more important. It is...

Consultants with real connections give very different feedback!

Make sure you understand that. I've seen consultants who unknowingly killed the most marketable parts of a screenplay. They truly don't understand what will sell a script, so they don't know that they just destroyed the writer's chance of success.

If you are trying to break into the industry, you need a reader who needs to maintain their REPUTATION with producers and agents, as well as screenwriters.

I'm not saying that consultants without connections don't provide value. Many are very good, and provide excellent notes on how to improve a script, but if you are ready to sell your screenplay, get consulting from someone who is connected.

Choosing a Script Consultant

The first step is the most important—get clear on your own needs. Are you looking for encouragement? If so, ask your network to recommend an encouraging consultant. Are you looking to improve your lead characters? Find a consultant who specializes in characters. Do you want to increase the marketability of your script? Then look for a consultant that focuses on marketability.

If you know what you need, you can find a consultant who specializes in that area. Or you can directly ask the consultant to focus on that area. But you're better off finding a specialist because they know that skill set inside and out.

Then get recommendations. Someone in your network has used consultants before. Ask them who they recommend... and who they don't recommend.

Here's a few questions to ask a script consultant:

- What are you best at? (Hopefully, that matches up with what you need.)

- Would you be willing to focus on ___(your primary need)_____ as you work with my script?

- What is your process? How do you give notes?

- Can I discuss the notes with you to get clarification?

Once they've done the job, then go through their comments and select the ones you want to apply to your script.

Remember, there are plenty of people who can point out typos and formatting problems, but a script consultant should add serious value to your script. You want them to discover important problems in a script and provide valuable solutions.

And if the consultant loves your script, they may recommend it to their contacts!

Strategy 17. Find a Mentor

Many of the top writers, producers, and actors credit their success to their relationship with their mentor. It is an excellent strategy for building your career and gaining a deeper understanding of the industry.

A mentor can make the difference you need to sell your screenplay and start your career.

In general, there are two types of mentors—paid mentors and volunteer mentors. There are advantages and disadvantages to each.

VOLUNTEER MENTORS

Advantage: These people have taken a personal interest in your career, and will sometimes risk their reputation for you.

Disadvantage: They're hard to find, and not always dependable. They are unpredictable in many ways. They can also drop you at the first sign of disagreement. And sometimes, they're overbearing.

To find a volunteer mentor, use the strategy below.

PAID MENTORS

Advantage: They are dependable, work on a schedule, and their primary purpose is moving writers through the journey. You know exactly what they are going to mentor you on, and you can hold them to that standard.

Disadvantage: You have to pay them.

For the best mentor I know of, go to **screenwritingu.com/ services**

STRATEGY FOR FINDING A MENTOR

In the ScreenwritingU Alumni, we have successful writers constantly mentoring new writers through an informal process. But if you are looking for a specific industry person to mentor you, try this process:

1. *Select someone appropriate to your level and to the task.* Don't go after A-list writers if you haven't written a screenplay yet. Instead, find someone who understands the next stage of your growth.

2. *Request mentorship on something specific.* Maybe it is on character creation or query letters or doing meetings. Just don't say, "I want you to mentor me through the whole screenwriting process." That sounds like a five-year job.

3. *If possible, ask for mentorship regarding a real industry event, like a meeting with a producer or an upcoming contest.* The more real the event, the more likely you'll get full participation from your mentor.

4. *Be as "low maintenance" as possible and be respectful of their time.* Remember, you're dealing with people who are very short on time. So the easier you make it for them, the better your chances.

5. *Once in the process, be coachable.* Listen and learn. If you're not going to be coachable, don't bother getting a mentor. It will just waste everyone's time.

6. *Don't pitch them on your project.* A mentor helps you learn, understand, and choose directions for your career. Don't make the mistake of trying to get them to produce your project or even trying to use their contacts... unless they offer.

Remember, the right advice at the right time can be the absolute key to success. So it is worth the effort to establish relationships with potential mentors.

RESOURCES:

Mentorship at ScreenwritingU
screenwritingu.com/services

Strategy 18. Call Production Companies

Most people think that only agents can get a script into a production company, but there are many production companies that will listen to pitches from writers. In general, they are the small producers and some mid-sized companies.

If you are outgoing, and enjoy talking to people, this may be one of your favorite strategies.

A few key points will help:

1. *Be calm.* Don't act like a used-car salesperson.

Think of them as someone just doing a job, and their job is to find great scripts... and to weed out the ones that don't work for their company.

2. *Know your pitch, and bring it down to one SIMPLE sentence.*

You need to be able to say your pitch in 8 to 10 seconds. You need to get the words out before they say "No unsolicited materials." It should be totally clear, and get to the essence of your story. If possible, it should be stated as a HOOK.

3. *Target your market.*

Most writers want to get their script to the very top of the industry, but don't have the credibility or experience to accomplish that. Studios and major production companies already have thousands of writers with proven track records. They also have legal concerns about working with new writers.

But there are over 5,000 small production companies who will listen to your pitch. Some of them are connected to the big boys, some have funds, but most importantly, they are hungry!

Find companies who: 1) do movies similar to yours, and 2) who have an open door. That's your market.

4. *Learn from their response.*

You'll pitch your concept, and they'll respond. They could get excited and request the script or they might ask questions or they might turn it down. Whatever they do, there's something valuable to learn from it—so your next pitch will be more successful.

5. *Keep moving until you find production companies who want to work with you.*

Once you've written a great script, created a great pitch, and targeted your market then it is all about the numbers. If you call 30 production companies, you'll be more successful than if you call two.

As always, keep at it until you succeed.

Strategy 19: Get An Agent

Almost every week, another one of our writers lands an agent or manager. So it is not the impossible dream that some say it is.

In the course of my interviews, I've talked with over 120 agents and managers here in Los Angeles about what causes them to sign a client.

Here's what I discovered. Having an agent is a "business relationship." You want them to sell screenplays and get you work in the industry. They want you to write screenplays that can easily be sold. That is a "business relationship." In order for the agent to sell screenplays, you've got to write MARKETABLE screenplays.

That's the deal.

How do you get an agent?

1. Start with a few high-quality and marketable screenplays.

2. Write a great query letter or pitch.

3. Do some quick research on IMDbPro.com to find managers and agents.

4. Send query letters or call with your pitch.

In general, managers are usually easier to get than agents, but in both cases, you need to bring value to the relationship. These people aren't volunteer mentors. They need to know that you will generate income, so the key is to bring in marketable screenplays.

Just keep in mind, agents and managers want to work with writers who are ready for the market. Take the time and effort necessary to build the quality of your screenplays and pitches, and you'll have much more success.

Do the right things and there will be an agent or manager in your future!

Chapter Five:
Strategies to Get More Connections

With each new person you add to your network, you create opportunities for their network to read your script.

Here are some untapped networking opportunities that could shift the odds in your favor.

Strategy 20. Intern With A Producer or Agency

Many of the top screenwriters and producers got their start by interning. They volunteered time and did the small jobs around the office and in exchange for that, they got to be part of the process of making deals in this industry.

Whether you intern, get a job, or even move up the ladder of a production company, you will be able to learn so much about this business just by seeing their day-to-day activities.

PRODUCERS VERSUS PRODUCTION?

There are two sides to this business—the agency/producer side and the production side. The first makes the deal; they are the ones that option and sell spec scripts to studios. The second does the physical production, turning the script into a movie.

If you are a writer who wants to sell a script, you'll want to intern at the places where those deals are made. The easiest path to success here is to start out at the kind of company that fits your screenplay—both for budget and genre.

Again, agencies and producers are both are focused on the business side of buying screenplays and getting them produced. Right now, that is your primary goal—to sell a screenplay. For this strategy, let's concentrate on producers.

WHAT YOU'LL LEARN

On my first day at a big producer's office (12 years ago), I was required to read over 200 query letters and report to the producer. I chose 4 scripts to request, but was instantly challenged about whether they fit this company or not. Ultimately, she allowed me to request two scripts out of 200 query letters. That was the moment I realized how important a solid pitch is to getting your script read.

You'll also learn:

- How the submission process works.

- What causes producers to request a script.

- What a producer's needs are.

- What causes a producer to option a script.

- How the development process works.

Throughout your internship, you'll get real life experience about how the business works, what producers buy and don't buy, who to go to with your screenplay, how to make your presentation, and many other vital pieces of information that can help you sell a script.

Of course, you'll also make connections that can pay off on your next script. Is it worth it to "give away your time" to a producer or agency? Without a doubt.

To find internships, Google "internship at production company."

Strategy 21. Work on Movie Productions

Now let's look at the value that can come from volunteering on movie productions.

From a "selling your script" perspective, the big value you get is making connections with low budget filmmakers. Of course, the producer and director will become connections for you, but you'll discover that the cast and crew are filled with filmmakers who are making other movies. Any of them can become connections to help you get your movie made.

So you get experience, connections, and possibly even a credit. It matures you because you get to see the production side of a movie being made.

Very likely, somewhere within 100 miles of you, a movie will soon be made and there are movie projects being organized on the Internet that you can be part of, also.

Filmmakers could need you for any of the following:

- Rewrite or polish their script

- Crew

- Catering

- Location scout

- Casting/acting

- Make Up

- Assistant to the producer or director

- Public Relations

- Social Networking

- Kickstarter campaign

- Marketing the movie

- Or 100 other things

Volunteering doesn't mean you are lower than anyone else. It means you are part of the team. Go there to help them succeed, thus making yourself valuable to everyone you meet on the set.

BTW, assume everyone there has a chance at success in this industry. The person cleaning the set today may be next year's breakout director. Work with them. Make friends. Then go back to them when you have your next script ready.

Strategy 22. Volunteer at a Conference or Charity Event with Producers

It is valuable to go to conferences and make connections there, but it is even more valuable if you are a volunteer at that event. Why? Because you are behind the scenes and seen as a resource to producers and celebrities.

Because of that, you get unprecedented access to major connections!

Think about it this way. Many conferences feature producers. Charity events in L.A. often have celebrities as special guests. And the best news is that conferences and events always need volunteers.

Remember, this is a business of ongoing relationships. We've had many of our writers make strong connections this way -- and some of those lead to deals.

Here is a list of the main events where this strategy works:

- Screenwriting conferences.

- Film Festivals.

- Social charity events that draw industry people.

- Fundraisers for industry causes—like restoring silent films.

- Political events specifically for the industry.

If you're in L.A. or New York, start looking for events that draw industry people. If you're outside of L.A., look for conferences and film festivals that happen in your area. Volunteer and you'll meet people who can become part of your network.

A friend of mine used this strategy with great success. He volunteered at charity events and quickly became the person who escorted the celebrities to the "green room." He made a point to send the celebs a thank you note and connect with them. After a while, he started connecting producers with actors, and built some very strong relationships.

Of course, he didn't start those relationships by trying to give celebrities his script the first time he saw them. Your priority is to be the best volunteer ever. Then as you build the relationship, let them know that you are a screenwriter, and things will develop from there.

Volunteering is a very positive way to stand out from the crowd.

Chapter Six:
Strategies to Get Outside Your
House/Comfort Zone

Starting to feel comfortable marketing your screenplay? Great! Now, let's get out of the house and do some face-to-face marketing.

Meeting people at industry events can give you some excellent connections to follow up on. Taking them to lunch creates even better relationships.

Strategy 23. Go to Live Pitch Fests

Getting face-to-face with a producer provides numerous benefits. First, it is easier to build relationships for future business. It is easier to gauge what works for them and what doesn't. And you can gain new insights into the business with each face-to-face contact.

Usually, in a single day, you have the chance to pitch five to fifteen different production companies, and sometimes more. So it is a great opportunity.

The beauty of a Pitch Fest is that every production company there is looking for new material and will listen with "willing ears."

Here's how it works:

Usually, you stand in line, waiting your turn to pitch someone from the production company. Once it is your turn, you get 5 minutes to pitch anything you'd like.

With each pitch, follow this simple and effective strategy:

1. Assume they are your friends and introduce yourself in one sentence.

2. Tell the genre and title.

3. Give a short pitch that hooks them.

4. Answer any questions they have.

Success comes from two things: *the concept you are pitching*, and *the quality of your pitch.*

If a producer doesn't like one project, just go on to your next script and pitch away. In this business, there is no rejection. Either you have what they want or you don't. It is never personal.

Of course, if they like your pitch, they'll request the script.

One last piece of advice: preparation is the key to success. Make sure you have a pitch that is short, to the point, and interesting. Practice your pitch on friends for a few days in advance. You want to go in feeling confident and knowing that your pitch is compelling. A little practice can help in both areas.

Strategy 24. Attend Film Festivals to Meet Filmmakers

Imagine a place where producers, directors, and even film distributors are eager to meet you and hang out. Sounds amazing, right?

Film festivals are the Hollywood away from Hollywood. They are the place where industry people go to relax and enjoy themselves. Besides parties, new releases are shown, and deals are made.

And you can be part of it!

Luckily, there are film festivals all over the world.

WHAT CAN YOU ACCOMPLISH AT A FILM FESTIVAL?

There's lots to be learned about marketing a movie and how audiences respond to independent films. It is also an easy place to meet filmmakers and build relationships.

Everyone is there to schmooze and networking can be done anywhere within a film festival. Here are a few suggestions:

- While standing in line for a film.

- Talk with them after a movie has played.

- Ask questions during the Q&A.

- At the bar at night.

- Over lunch.

- Attend the scheduled parties.

- At the panels.

- Even in the bathroom!

In fact, the person buying a burger next to you may be a producer. If so, strike up a conversation and see where it leads.

But don't lead with, "Hey, can you read my script?" This is about creating relationships and building your network. Ask them something about them or their experience of the festival. If you do a great job of that, your script will become part of the conversation in time.

Lastly, when you're at a film festival, go with the flow and be part of the event. Do that and you'll fit in and make more connections.

Strategy 25. Join Industry Groups with Professionals in their Membership

Where can you find hundreds of Industry professionals who will talk with you?

There are plenty of film industry organizations you can join. With organizations like Women in Film, Scriptwriter's Network, WGA, Independent Film Project, and others, it is always possible to meet someone new in the industry.

The key is to make sure there are actual "professionals" in the group. Why professionals? Because when an organization caters to professionals, the level of service and activities will be higher. Also, a group with professionals will attract more professionals while you are a member. So the business networking will be at a higher level.

Once you get into some of these organizations, here are some ways to determine if they'll further your career:

- Do they have professionals in the group?

- Do they bring in speakers from the industry?

- Do they have content that fits with your future?

- Is this a peer group that you'll benefit from?

- Can you contribute value to this group?

To find groups in your town, simply Google words like, "screen-writing groups, filmmaker groups, film industry" combined with the name of your city or state.

Now, your job is to visit some of these organizations to see which ones work best for you.

RESOURCES:

Hollywood Networking Breakfast
ChangingImagesInAmerica.org

FilmIndependent
filmindependent.org

WomenInFilm (L.A., Seattle, Vancouver, Dallas, Chicago, and many other cities.)
wif.org

Strategy 26. Come to L.A. for Industry Events

L.A. is filled with industry events and you can plan a trip here at almost any time of the year to meet producers, actors, directors, and other industry players.

The easiest way to do this is to select the events you'd like to attend while in town. Schedule a week around those events, and book meetings for the rest of the week.

With more than 30 award shows a year in L.A., you can put on a Tux and hob-nob with the stars on multiple occasions. For two to three months before the Academy Awards, there are big industry events almost every week.

If you schedule it well, you can fill your time with meetings, award shows, and visits to different screenwriting organizations.

Here's some of the events that happen regularly in Los Angeles:

- Big Award Shows: WGA, DGA, PGA, Los Angeles Film Critics, etc.

- Conferences: Produced By Conference, Show Biz Expo, etc.

- Festivals: L.A. Film Festival, L.A. Comedy Shorts Film Festival, etc.

- Market: American Film Market.

- Screenings with the producer, director, and actors speaking after the movie.

- Networking events: Hollywood Networking Breakfast and others.

But they don't just happen in L.A.; there are a series of legitimate award shows around the country. There are also major film and TV events that happen in Las Vegas and NYC.

But you'll benefit greatly from spending a week in L.A. meeting people and attending Industry events.

RESOURCE:

Site lists up-to-date industry events in multiple cities:
industryhappenings.com

Strategy 27. Set up a Public Read-through and Invite Industry People

Imagine having a room full of industry people listen as actors read your screenplay. People laugh at the right parts, sit spellbound during the suspenseful parts, and applaud vigorously at the end. What a great way to present your masterpiece!

Who put this event together? *You did.*

Here's how:

First, of course, you need to make sure your script is absolutely amazing. You don't want this strategy backfiring on you. So before you ever invite a single industry player, have a private read-through where you can get feedback and make sure your script does well in this medium.

Then follow these simple steps:

1. *Get a location.*

There are theaters, auditoriums, library meeting rooms, and many other places that will do just fine for a read-through. Make some calls and you may be surprised at the variety and the different prices offered for these rooms. And if possible, select a location that has a lot of production companies in the neighborhood.

2. *Get actors to read the parts.*

What actors do you know? If you can get one of them on board, they may bring ten of their actor friends. Another strategy is to go to a local acting troupe who wants exposure. It is just as valuable for them to be in front of a group of industry players as it is for you. For the price of a pizza and beer party, you may be able to get a stage full of actors.

3. *Have a rehearsal.*

This is essential... even if it is done two hours before the actual read-through. The rehearsal will get the bugs out, have people feel more comfortable with the screenplay, and just as important, it will tell you who is going to really show up for your read-through. Remember, if there aren't actors on the stage, no one gets to experience your script.

What if certain actors don't show up? Be prepared with a list of alternates. Get on your cell phone and start calling.

4. *Invite industry people.*

Invite anyone you think has a connection to a potential buyer. An assistant or even an intern can be as good as having a producer there. If the assistant falls in love with your script, her producer won't stop hearing about it.

Use email, phone calls, and faxes to invite industry people. The rule here is "Invite 50 to get 20." So don't stop when the room capacity is full. If the event overflows, it will give the impression of a huge success.

5. *Fill the room with people who love your work.*

If you expect to have 20 people from production companies, then fill the rest of the room with fans of your work. Why? Because producers will remember the audience response. Raving fans = box office success.

CAUTION: This is not a strategy to use to get feedback. Don't do this one unless your screenplay is absolutely amazing and you have confirmation from someone inside the business who says so. If you have industry people in the room, it is because your script is already amazing.

The key: *Get feedback from non-buyers and get a sale from the buyer.*

Strategy 28: Breakfast, Lunch, and Dinner

This is a great strategy to use once you've made initial contact with a producer, assistant, or development executive. And it fits how business is done inside this industry.

You simply get on the phone, call the person you've met, and ask them to breakfast, lunch or dinner. This isn't a date and it isn't a pitch session. It is a chance to get to know each other, learn more about how they do what they do, and build the relationship.

Once you've built that relationship, then you are free to contact them with your scripts in the future.

TO FOLLOW-UP ON A FIRST CONTACT

You may email or call and let them know that you are going to be in town. If possible, you'd like to have lunch or dinner so you can get to know them a bit better. It is that easy.

LOCATION MATTERS

Make sure you find a restaurant near their office. If possible, within walking distance. Los Angeles is spread out so much, if you pick a restaurant outside their neighborhood, it can become a two hour ordeal for them to drive to and from the location.

You could say, "I'd be happy to meet you near your office. Any place that works well for you?"

THE MEETING

Do your homework. Know who they are and what is on their slate.

Over the course of the meal, you may discuss the kind of things you talk about with friends. Sports, kids, politics, etc. You may ask them how they got started, what they like most about this business, what their goals are for the future -- and be prepared to answer the same questions. You'll also discuss the business, projects they have going on, and industry events that are coming up. Somewhere in there, you'll establish a relationship.

If they ask you about your current project, have a short pitch (1 or 2 sentences) that is interesting and instantly causes them to see the movie. Answer any questions, but don't push it on them during this meeting. However, if they request the script, send it to them.

Naturally, you'll pick up the check. But you will get so much value in return. The contact itself is tremendously valuable, but you also will learn about the industry... and the more you know, the more effective you can be at your next meeting.

IF YOU ARE MORE ADVENTUROUS, YOU MIGHT TRY...

... using this strategy to meet producers, execs, and assistants for the first time.

This might be out of your comfort zone. But if you are outgoing, friendly, and not a stalker, this might be a perfect way to build a network.

I learned this strategy from Bonnie Orr, a successful screenwriter from Austin, Texas.

Over a period of two years, she shared a meal with hundreds of producers, development execs and assistants. Those connections turned into relationships and some of those turned into screenplay sales. Obviously, you can do this inside L.A. or NYC, but you can also do it with your local film community.

CAUTION: Do not cross over into stalker mode. Have something to pitch that fits their market, but don't pitch it until you are asked. Then, give a short pitch and KNOW WHEN TO STOP TALKING.

Just as important, have fun with this! You never know who is going to become a key player in your future.

Strategy 29. Produce or Direct Your Own Movie

Producing or directing your own movie is one of the ultimate networking strategies. Most people would focus entirely on the "work-at-hand," not recognizing all of the other benefits that come from this amazing venture.

Consider these benefits:

Experience

- Brings a new reality to your writing.

- Know what works and doesn't on a set.

- Communicate with production people.

- Understand the needs of producers, directors, and actors.

Credibility

- IMDb credit.

- People will see that you follow through and complete a project.

- Introduce yourself as "I'm (name) and I've produced a movie."

- What you say will be credible.

- Festival recognition.

Using your film as an event to network

- As you are casting and crewing up, use this to connect with people.

- Have a screening and invite industry people.

- Go to a festival with a film and you stand out.

- Post your short or movie on YouTube.

- Send out press releases.

- Post on every social media outlet you're on.

Thinking past this movie to your future

- Use this experience to set up connections for the future.

- Start preparing the cast and crew for your next movie.

- Have the next script ready to promote to producers.

Ready for the great news? You don't have to shoot an entire feature film to get those benefits. You can shoot a short. Use it to market your work and submit it to festivals.

The movie *LOOPER* started as a treatment... that was turned into a short... that was then turned into a feature film. See that treatment here. **rcjohnso.com/Looper/looperorig.pdf**

Of course, you could shoot the feature film, with the added benefit that your script has been turned into an actual movie.

Whatever you choose, make sure it is the best it can be—especially the script. So many people rush into production with an average script and then end up with a below-average movie.

Get the script right and you'll have a great movie—that will build a great network!

Chapter Seven:
Strategies to Launch
on Other Platforms

Less than a decade ago, a screenplay could only be used as the foundation for a movie.

But all of that has changed.

Your screenplay can be used as source material to be launched on multiple platforms, some of which can help get your movie made; and some can make you famous!

Strategy 30. Create a Web Series

Some stories can be turned into a Web series. In that case, you use the original script as source material. It is easy to think of certain scenes as episodes. The difference is that each episode must have a beginning, middle, and end -- with a cliff hanger at the conclusion.

Two amazing things will happen for you when you come out with episodes every week. First, you'll discover what has to happen to keep an audience engaged. That will influence how you write every episode and every script from now on. Second, you will become really good at building a fan base—which will become your network for future projects.

THE PROCESS

1. *Write the series.*

   - You need a hook that will draw an audience.

   - Create a Season Arc.

   - Episodes have a beginning, middle, and end.

2. *Produce it.*

   - Episodes are often short—2 to 10 minutes.

   - Set up to continuously produce episodes.

   - Use actors who are totally committed and will remain with the project.

3. Market it to build a fan base.

- Create a web site, FB, Twitter, blog, etc.

- Send out press releases.

- Notify your social networks about every episode.

- Enter contests and festivals.

- Get a YouTube channel.

- Get your cast and crew to promote it to their networks.

It is easy to get lost in the writing and production. Just keep reminding yourself that the real purpose here is to build a fan base, keep your audience engaged, and to use this project to get your stories in front of producers.

Every episode is another chance to promote yourself, your writing, and your future!

Strategy 31. Kindle Your Screenplay

You've created an amazing story filled with wonderful characters, now what if you could make it so popular online that producers would come to you?

You can do that by novelizing your script and putting it on Kindle!

This doesn't mean that you put your screenplay into a .pdf and sell it. It means that you use your screenplay as an outline for a light novel. This also gives you the added advantage of having an "underlying property" that makes your screenplay more attractive to producers.

But the most important job here is to build a fan base for your writing. Producers are looking for built-in audiences that increase the chance that a movie will succeed at the box office. If the book takes off, you'll have real evidence that your screenplay can be a hit!

How do you create your fan base... thus expanding the power of your own network?

Create excitement with your current network.

Build a fan page on Facebook and get everyone you know on it.

Get reviews from your fans to get your book rated highly.

Use "book tours on blogs" to build popularity.

Do interviews wherever possible online.

If you've got a great network, they can drive that book to #1 in a market niche. Then, you'll use that as bait to get producers to read your book for a potential movie. Just put the words "Best Selling Novel" in the subject line, with a pitch and link in the body of the email.

With each of these steps, you are building your brand as a great storyteller. In time, that will create demand across multiple markets.

Strategy 32. Change the Medium

There are so many ways that a story can be told today. While many stories were originally created for just one medium, they could easily be switched to another market and may be more successful.

Think about your own story. Could it be told through one of these mediums?

- Episodic TV series

- HBO mini-series

- Netflix Original Series

- Comic book

- Graphic novel

- Video game

- Web Series

- Novel

- Or some new medium that doesn't exist today

What this is about is changing markets. Why? Because a project that doesn't find traction in one market may be embraced by another. Once it has success in that market, it may cross over back to the original you had intended.

But you want to make thoughtful decisions here. Some writers try to write the same project in five different mediums and end up wasting years of their lives on a single script. I've also heard producers tell new writers to turn their script into a novel, not because it was what was best for the story, but because that was the business model they use—optioning books and adapting them into movies.

Slow down. Make the best decision for you and your business model. When this strategy works, it is because you found a "home" for your story. It is because you found the right medium for this story in this time.

But what does it really take to switch markets?

You'll need to learn the rules of the new market and the players. Our production company was well versed in the features market, but when we went into the Reality TV market, we found both familiar and unfamiliar rules for doing business. We also had to build an entirely new network of business associates.

Of course, different markets have different entry requirements. To get a script read by a producer, you just need a recommendation, a great pitch or query letter, and a script. To get a TV pilot read by a network, you often need a showrunner, a series bible with two to five seasons mapped out, and an amazing pilot script.

You also need to research the potential market to see what has a future and what is dying out. Right now, Netflix is very hot. Graphic novels were the craze three years ago, but seem to have cooled down. So make sure the direction you take can get you where you want to go.

Remember, this isn't the first strategy you try. Give your screen-play its best chance before you make a major move like this.

However, switching mediums and/or markets could be the strat-egy that changes everything for you... as long as it is done because it gives your story the best possible home in this moment.

Strategy 33. Create a Plan and Seize the Opportunities!

Of all the 33 strategies for breaking into Hollywood, this one could be the most valuable.

Create a plan ASAP and implement it!

This can be as easy as picking the three or four strategies you'll put into place in the next month. Or you can use this set of strategies to build a long-term plan that has one strategy working into the next.

But don't let a day go by without creating a plan.

Once you start using these strategies, opportunities will come your way. How often those opportunities show up will depend upon the quality of your hooks, the amount of promotion you do, and the quality of your writing.

The key is to *Seize the Opportunities*!

Too many times, people have opportunities, but either don't recognize them or fritter them away. Sometimes, people freeze up when they have a star or producer in front of them. Sometimes, they are confused by the conflicting advice their friends give them.

Instead, you'll seize the day. You'll realize that you generated this opportunity and you deserve it. You'll step up to the plate and swing away. And then you'll enjoy the newfound success that has come from all the work you did.

Here are a couple of tips:

- Create opportunities through great writing and consistent marketing.

- Look for opportunities that emerge as you market yourself.

- Go with the opportunities that show up.

- Don't hide from opportunities.

- Be great at the critical moments!

Commit to the process. Commit to doing the work. Prepare. Then embrace the opportunities that come your way. Do that and you'll have a great life!

Now, go forth and take full advantage of the opportunities that come your way!

Conclusion

Knowledge is important. Action gives knowledge real meaning. Successful action can change your life.

You've now seen the list of 33 Ways to sell your screenplay. Obviously, you knew many of these before you bought this book, but I have a question for you.

How many of the 33 Ways have you applied in the last month?

If you haven't marketed yourself in the last month, don't feel bad. This book is the chance to find the inspiration, learn a set of skills, and know that it is possible for you to break into this industry.

But of all the strategies listed here, #1 You Need Great Writing and #3 Make Sure It is Marketable are the most important. Quality and marketability are the keys to making all the other strategies work.

And you can do it!

At least once a week, we have another SU Alumni writer make a deal. You can see those here ScreenwritingU.com/success-stories . The reason I mention that is that those 300 deals are proof that anyone... from any country... at any age... can make a screenplay deal.

You now have a list of 33 Ways to Sell Your Screenplay. Make sure you watch the video on how to create your own "Screenplay Marketing Campaign using 33 Ways!" at: 33WaysBook.com

If you need motivation or coaching or improved writing, come join us at ScreenwritingU.

In all that you do, I wish you the best!

Hal Croasmun
President
ScreenwritingU

P.S.: Please give us a positive rating on Amazon. If for some reason you don't like something about this book, let me know and we'll improve it. Just contact us at: support.screenwritingu.com and let me know what the problem is. We'll take care of you.

Resources
That Can Change Your Life

This list includes some of the resources ScreenwritingU provides to screenwriters:

SOCIAL NETWORKING

ScreenwritingU on Twitter: twitter.com/ScreenwritingU

ScreenwritingU on Facebook: facebook.com/ScreenwritingU

FREE SCREENWRITING CLASSES
screenwritingu.com/class-list/free

Every month, Hal Croasmun does at least one free class either on a teleconference or webinar. These are real classes that cover important subjects like, "How to Get an Agent."

DOWNLOAD OSCAR NOMINATED SCREENPLAYS

screenwritingu.com/download-oscar-nominated-screenplays

Over 70 screenplays from the 2011 - 1014 are available for legal download.

TOP 30-DAY CLASSES

screenwritingu.com/class-list/10-30-day

In 30 days, you can make a leap in these important areas:

How to Write a Screenplay in 30 Days with the Mini-Movie Method

The Profound Screenwriter

PROSERIES PROFESSIONAL SCREENWRITING PROGRAM

screenwritingu.com/classes/proseries-professional-screenwriting-program

Learn 300 essential screenwriting skills in 6 months. This is an intense Boot Camp that prepares you to work with producers.

MASTER SCREENWRITER CERTIFICATE PROGRAM

screenwritingu.com/classes/master-screenwriter-certificate

The most advanced Master class in existence. In this 14 month program, you are coached through the process of marketing two screenplays. (Must complete ProSeries first).

46884222R00060

Made in the USA
Middletown, DE
02 June 2019